Watergate 2.0

The Manchurian President? Trump's Radical Transformation of American Politics

By

Eric Engle

Copyright © 2017

http://mindworks.altervista.org

INTRODUCTION

I wrote this book to help you understand the revolutionary changes President Trump brings to American politics so you can be a better citizen and investor: so you can understand the risks, opportunities, and long term trends President Trump's administration augurs.

I studied law in the USA, France, and Germany and have taught law in many countries. I speak several languages fluently. I have authored dozens of law review articles and many books about law and politics. I won a Fulbright scholarship, and worked at Harvard Law School as a researcher. All of that puts me in a good position to provide unique insights to the American political scene that you might not otherwise get.

I want this book to inspire you to live up to the *ideals* Trump proclaims, regardless of what you think of Trump the person or President: those ideals are universal and timeless. As to policy, I want you to understand why the USA has so many social problems and to see Trump, for good or ill, as a reaction to that. I think this will make you a better citizen and will help build a better world.

Table of Contents

Forward!

In this book I use the rough language of politics, not the refined language of diplomacy, because I am talking about US domestic politics and because I think that makes you likelier to read and remember what I say here. Politics, also known as "alt war" really is the alternative to open violence: the ballot or the bullet. Some of my words here might be bluff or bluster; the tone or accent might not be as sharp or as gentle as ought exactly be. However, whether right or wrong, whether over-stated or under-stated, the opinions and ideas I express herein are my own and what I truly believe likely to be the case.

"We know how to save the Union. The world knows we do know how to save it. We -- even we here -- hold the power, and bear the responsibility. In giving freedom to the slave, we assure freedom to the free -- honorable alike in what we give, and what we preserve. We shall nobly save, or meanly lose, the last best hope of earth."

-Abraham Lincoln

Introduction

Trump radically transformed US politics from a bi-partisan consensus of free trade, open immigration, and frequent foreign military intervention. He is replacing those policies with economic nationalism, militarist isolationism, and limiting immigration. Trump shattered *both* major political parties. Trump presents an ideological transformation. The ideological transformation Trump presents coincides with the splintering and fragmentation of *both* major political parties. Whatever Trump's personal fate, the transformation of American party politics, economic policy, and foreign policy is undeniable and deep, with implications beyond Trump's term of office, however long or brief it may be. The implications concern *both* major political parties and *all* Americans, both North and South.

No matter what, Trump's domestic political realignment will prove to be as revolutionary as Reagan's, perhaps even as deep a transformation as that worked by Franklin Roosevelt. In the 2016 election Trump easily captured *all* swing states *as well as* winning states like Michigan and Wisconsin. States which traditionally always voted Democrat due to their (long gutted) labor union base. These "blue collar" states flipped and voted the Republican economic nationalist, Donald Trump into office. Trump champions economic nationalism and government economic intervention, which is a radical rupture from the bipartisan policy consensus of globalization and laissez faire capitalism which preceded him.

Trump also rejects neoconservative unilateral military interventions, because they brought chaos and death to most of the Islamic world with no improvement in the safety and well-being of ordinary Americans, to say nothing of the soldiers, sailors, airmen and marines who bear the price in blood of endless war. Trump's foreign policy is thus also a radical rupture. Trump, decried as an extremist, seeks simply to work a generally prudent consolidation of American power on the basis of international relations realism. Trump broke the lying teeth of neocon vampires who were sucking the blood of innocent Arabs and American heroes alike to further their crusade of chaos for profit. Instead of "nation building" and endless avoidable foreign military interventions, Trump seeks to do fewer things abroad, but hopefully better.

These are all major policy changes for the Republican party. The GOP had championed policies of free-trade, selective but open immigration, and foreign military intervention. All of those ideas are now in the dust-bin, at least so far as the Republican party is concerned, given Trump's sweeping victory at the electoral college and the fact he carried more than one traditional bastion of the democratic party.

President Trump's foreign and domestic policies – economic nationalism and foreign policy realism - are most akin to those of Nixon. "The reality President" always generates controversy. Yet, Trump may also be like Nixon in facing scandal - his efforts to scapegoat Moslems may instead end with him as the scapegoat for fat cats and oligarchs.

These are the topics for this small book: the radical changes Trump has wrought, and whether and how they might end in a splintering of American political parties and the possible downfall of Trump himself.

CHAPTER I.
DECLINE AND DISINTEGRATION OF THE TWO POLITICAL PARTIES: PHOENIX OR PINATA?

Both major American parties are going through a death dance.

This death dance of the major political parties is largely incomprehensible to non-elites or even to foreign elites. I compare this dance to the rise of a Phoenix or the fall of a Pinata: Either one or both parties will transform themselves yet again and thereby remain "big tent" parties able to take in, at least theoretically, each American and rise like a phoenix to carry all Americans ever upward.[1] Or, instead, one or both of the major parties will shatter or splinter, resulting in the formation of new major American political parties like a broken pinyata scattering too little candy too widely for any to be satisfied leaving only colorful broken bits as evidence of broken promises of wealth for all. On this splintering the next decades' political future will turn.

This is not the first time by any means that the main political parties have transformed. However, a simultaneous transformation of ideology and policy this broad and deep affecting *both* major parties at the same time is a truly once-in-a-lifetime event, marking generations and the political landscape of Gerrmandy. The implications, contours, and exact extent of this transformation in progress remain entirely uncertain, not the least due to the cloud of scandal hanging over the Showman in Chief Trump.

If the democrats splinter further they will wind up as Green Ecologists (led by Stein) and/or Red Socialists (led by

---

1 The phoenix is regarded by some, including perhaps a few free-masons, as the esoteric symbol of the American eagle, the hidden meaning behind the visual image. But in truth the American eagle is none other than the watchful warning eagle placed atop the tree of peace of the Haudenosaunee (Iroquois), who will warn the native nations of any impending danger. The ideas of the Haudenosaunee (Iroquois) about federalism influenced the American republic so much that their symbol is now the symbol of the new republic, bearer of the message of Dekanawidah, the Peace-giver. Likewise the clutch of arrows is also both a symbol of the Haudenosaunee (Iroquois) confederacy and of the US federation.

Sanders), with the remainder constituting a rump Democratic party, probably led by Clintonistas, Obama, or an uneasy alliance of both, depending on whether "Organizing for Action" defects into another splinter or instead remains part of the rump democrats. None of these three – or more - parties would likely be able to muster the voters and ideology needed to capture the white house. Whether and how new parties could form coalitions at the national, i.e. federal level is a vital, interesting, and unanswered speculation.

It is also possible, though less likely, that the Republicans (too?) will splinter into 1) an unfunded and likely violent ultra right party composed of white-nationalist neo-nativists, quasi-fascists, "alt-right" Putinistas and/or 2) libertarians leaving 3) a free-trade open-immigration finance-capital rump Republican party.

In other words: People who call the US President "President Rump" may be right, but if they are it is for the wrong reasons.

The Democrats are likelier to Splinter than the Republicans. This is because the democratic "rainbow" base is more diverse than the republican rich white man's club: the competing interests of various minorities, workers, and alternative economists are why why the Democrats are likelier to splinter. Further points of fracture follow the lines of identity politics: diverse interesters of groups split by age, sex, and race. The Democrats are also likelier to splinter because the democrats already have Green Ecologist and Social Democratic "parties within the party", *Fraktionen*, parties which the national democrats evidently don't quite know just what to do with. For example, Sanders, who is not a democrat, was allowed to present himself as a Democratic presidential candidate, which is ridiculous on its face.

The rise of Trump can partly be understood as a result of the decline of the republican party. In 2016 the republicans proved unable to field a more palatable candidate who could win the general election. Both parties fielded bad candidates in 2016, unlike 2008: In 2008 both parties fielded very good candidates, just as they did back in 1992. That means that the current incapacity of *either* party to field a winning candidate who is also a good candidate, is not due to the demographic and political shocks the USA has faced since 2000. Bad candidates are the result of factionalized zero-sum politics which forgot bi-partisanship, the Weimarization of America. To show the level of intra-party friction in the Republican party: the retired former Speaker of the House accused the candidate Cruz, famous for the attempted shut-down of the U.S. government, of being "Lucifer in the flesh", literally demonizing a fellow citizen. I might well disagree with candidate Cruz, perhaps even dislike him as a person: but I would nonetheless be civil toward him. That's civic prudence, a basic virtue needed for a functioning democracy. I guess that doesn't sell advertising, motivate the base, or split the opposition? Why don't the so-called leaders lead by good example?

Have none of you read Federalist #10 ?

Fantasies to the contrary, Cruz is in fact (stand back) *a person.* Shocking, I know. Candidates today polarize, which they might be obliged to do in a primary, but they do not unite after the primary – which they must do whether they are elected or lost, at least if the USA is to be a healthy liberal democracy.

The former speaker, in contrast, referred to Trump as a former golf partner. Golf is a sport generally played by wealthy white people. Even this attempt at conciliation thus failed as a national measure of the greatness of the candidate: America is not populated exclusively by wealthy white people.

Ah, politics...

So, part of the republicans inability to field an attractive electable Presidential candidate may be due to the fact that the republican base is white wealthy non-immigrants.

Inner party splintering, fractious conflict, polarization, failure to unify, is *not* unique to the republicans. For example, speaker Boehner referred to Obama's king-maker role, saying: ***"Don't be shocked ... if two weeks before the convention, here comes Joe Biden parachuting in and Barack Obama fanning the flames to make it all happen"***

Boehner pointed that out because Hilary Clinton illegally used her personal email server instead of a secured state department issued server. This in turn could have led Clinton to be forced out of the race at the last minute by Biden, or a Biden-Clinton struggle at the democratic convention. It is underlying scandal, product of complacent corruption, that creates conditions for factionalization. Biden did nto in fact "parachute in at the last minute". Clinton's server scandal was not so bad as to force Clinton into a last minute negotiation or resignation. That ended Obama's kingmaker role: Obama wound up supporting Clinton, but ineffectually. Instead, Clinton's digital irregularities resulted in a criminal investigation, the existence of which was published just days prior to the election: October Surprise. Comey's publication of that investigation likely decided the election - though Russian interference could have contributed as well.

It is this cloud of Russian influence in the election which scandalizes President Trump, and plays into certain flaws in his team and leadership style. However, to understand the disintegration and factionalization of American inter-party politics we must look first at the failure of Clinton: for it as not merely the FBI nor Russian interference which cost her the election.

A. *Why Did Clinton Blow It? An Analysis of 2016*

Many Democrats have trouble accepting the ugly truth: their candidate sucked, so she lost. The proper question isn't to blame Trump, or the voters but to ask what Clinton did wrong that lost "her" election?

Bitter Grounds: Syria, Libya...

This is a strong black cup of STFU,
you unprincipled opportunistic elitist egotist.

It wasn't just entitled arrogance, and dishonesty which cost Clinton the election. Nor was it Russian meddling. It was also Trump's strategy and tactics which won him the election.

One of the many ways the 2016 election was unusual was because the Republicans were able to contest even New York State, which is one of the most solidly democratic states in federal presidential elections. Trump has strong connections with New York state, which enabled him to contest it. Yet, the election was bitter not only because each of the candidates was deep in New York and fought tooth-and-nail for that populous state. It was also bitter because Trump is a loudmouth reality star, a shock jock, whereas Clinton is a feminist: those are basic cultural opposites. Each of them waged a hard-hitting campaign using language which Chinese élites would likely find incomprehensibly rude, especially in a political context among contenders claiming to be worthy of leadership, leaders claiming to be rational decision makers articulating the national interest and mediating domestic conflict.

Although there was much dirty campaign tactics and mudslinging, the fraudulent aspects of the 2016 election, Russian interference, were less evident than those of 2000. Frankly, Gore was weak and indecisive about driving home voter fraud in 2000, unlike Clinton in 2016. Even if Russian efforts to influence the election were at all effective they could never have won the election for Trump without Clinton's errors.

Although the campaign was bitter and hard-fought with sharp political infighting, dire predictions to the contrary there have in fact been just about no politically motivated riots, assassinations, or street-fighting since, the portents of doom some seek to invoke and stoke. America today is not Germany in the 1930s with freebooters and communists waging open warfare in the streets. Trump can always use patriotism as a way to unleash and restrain his more violent supporters, reminding them that they are *Americans* and should fight for their rights to be the best, and also at times reminding them that their opponents are also *Americans*. It is this potential to transcend partisan politics around

national unity which makes it possible to plausibly compare
Trump to Reagan. Reagan was largely *hated* from 1979
well into 1983 yet is only remembered for the last five years
of his term in which he became more and more popular.

Clinton and Trump are both good public speakers.
However, Trump proved marginally better. Worst for Clinton
is her lousy reputation: Clinton is considered to be be
dishonest, opportunistic, hypocritical, someone who would
say whatever it takes to get elected no matter what. This
can be seen from her flip-flops on gay marriage, black
crime, and free trade and most recently her defense of a
man named Franken.

Demographically Clinton's core base was white women and
Trump's core base is white men. Neither candidate drew or
repelled the rich as a class more than the other. The
republicans are normally the party of the wealthy, and the
democrats are normally the party of the poor. Clinton is the
"elite democrat" and Trump is the "commoner republican",
so their respective party affiliations canceled out their cross-
cutting class affiliation.

What about Blacks, Hispanics, East Asians, and South
Asians? Jews or Catholics? Age versus youth?Age-versus-
youth was fairly evident: younger people tended to vote for
Clinton, and older people tended to vote for Trump.

Catholic people were likelier to vote for Trump, because
Clinton cannot credibly oppose abortion rights. Jewish
people are likelier to vote for Clinton because they tend to
see themselves as intellectual and socially oriented. So,
even though some Hispanics voted for Clinton because of

immigration, others did not. This was one of the demographic holes in Clinton's strategy. The Hispanic voters were not solidly for Clinton, nor were women for that matter. Clinton's inability to excite and motivate youth or black people also was one factor costing Clinton the election. Black people proved to be a more interesting case. Trump won based on a coalition of disaffected white and black people coupled with a sector of the rich white elite. Plenty of black people are genuinely disaffected. Trump carried more black votes than expected, and more importantly many black people, like many youth, simply did not get out and vote. Many, even most black people are not fond of abortion because some black people correctly see that abortion rights is code for the slow soft genocide of the black nation: eugenics, Margaret Sanger style. Clinton's pro-abortion position, which she was constrained to take by gender and party cost her votes. If you look at the statistics, and I have, it is evident that abortion has the effect of population control: abortion rights keep the whites as a majority with respect to other races. Where we see an outcome it is not difficult to guess an intention. Perhaps this is why Obama was unable to rally black voters to get out and vote for Hillary. How much that is Obama's fault is an interesting question; I see no reason to ascribe low black voter turn-out to Obama.

A CATEGORICAL CLASS ANALYSIS OF TRUMP VERSUS CLINTON

RICH	**white**	**black**	**hispanic**	**asian**
	CATHOLIC	CATHOLIC	CATHOLIC	CATHOLIC
	Protestant	Protestant	Protestant	PROTESTANT
	Jewish	Jewish	Jewish	Jewish
	Other	Other	other	OTHER

POOR	**white**	**black**	**hispanic**	**ASIAN**
	CATHOLIC	CATHOLIC	CATHOLIC	CATHOLIC
	Protestant	Protestant	protestant	PROTESTANT
	Jewish	Jewish	Jewish	Jewish
	Other	Other	OTHER	OTHER

CAPITALS INDICATE A GROUP LIKELIER TO VOTE FOR TRUMP
Lower Case Indicates A Group Likelier To Vote For Clinton

What this table brings out is that Trump carried the the Catholic vote, even the catholic vote, whereas Clinton carried the non-religious Hispanic vote. Unfortunately for Clinton, most Hispanic people tend to take their religion a bit more seriously than white elite intellectuals. Asians, in contrast, tended to vote solidly for Trump on the logic of maintaining law and order and because of the idea of personal responsibility and success through hard-work, not largesse. Clinton could have better contested the Asian vote because East Asians tend to be intellectual, though some are religious. She could have better touted her Yale credentials and few but serious intellectual achievements: instead she largely ignored both East Asians and South

Asians. This is one meaning of the idea that Clinton is an entitled elitist.

This graph does not include youth/elderly because youth tend not to vote: Clinton's inability to energize and motivate the youth vote was one other demographic hole in the Clinton campaign.
This graph does not split by men/women because just as the elderly were likelier to vote for Trump but followed their family first, so also were women likelier to vote for Clinton but followed their family in the end. These generalizations enable us to get a picture that is roughly accurate.

Two classes, four races, and four religions creates 36 cells. For more complexity and accuracy add three ages (youth, middle aged, elderly) and two genders (men, women) which would results in 216 cells. Cast that across 50 states and we have 50*216 cells.

I have the intellectual ability to analyze the data for 1080 cells and then project that data through populations and states to determine which candidate will win the majority of votes and a rough prediction of the number of elector they will win at the electoral college. 2016 was yet another 51% election and split just like in 2000 such that the elected candidate won a minority of cast votes. To me the lesson is obvious: abolish the electoral college and make the election of the U.S. president by popular vote without regard to the states.

The **election was Clinton's to lose and she blew it.** She lose because she did not get a solid endorsement from **Obama,** which she needed to motivate the **Black** vote. She did not not campaign enough among among **Hispanics**, who are generally anti-abortion, nor did her campaign focus on capturing the **Asian** vote. Her strategy assumed demographics would inevitably win the election for her, that she would not have to motivate or even ask these constituencies for their support. Clinton failed to understand that a candidate *must* motivate groups of people to actually get out and vote for her. *The vote is not a mere poll!* You can win a poll and lose an election. Hi Hillary!

2016 could have been the first U.S. election decided by non-white voters: instead, Trump motivated white people and some minorities to actually get out and vote for him, unlike Clinton. The white vote was already largely determined due to class and gender. White Women of all classes and faiths generally voted for Clinton they did not vote for Clinton nor was their turn-out much higher than average. Clinton did not win the number of votes from women she expected. Why is that..?

White Men of all classes and faiths generally voted for Trump. Trump tried to split off Latinos and Blacks, who mostly voted for Clinton, but again did not do so in sufficient numbers. Trump was strategically shrewd with a campaign *intended* to win traditionally democratic states. Despite stating that this was his strategy during the campaign Clinton did not react. She didn't fall into his trap: it wasn't a trap. She did however walk right into it. Not only was Trump's strategy shrewd his tactics took their toll too. Trump constantly and consistently attacked Clinton as a lying, dishonest, hypocritical criminal, "crooked Hillary" and with focus groups he also tested smears Clinton as a pro-abortion baby-killer, anti-sex, anti-black, and anti-baby and released some of those attacks but focused on specific audiences those messages would appeal to. Trump has absolutely no problem staying "on message", Twiterati to the contrary. Since at least Reagan, leftists consistently misconstrue feigned republican stupidity for the real thing: republican candidates aren't stupid, they *act* that way to be popular.

Clinton, unlike Trump, was not aggressive. She failed to attack Trump aggressively and repeatedly for fraud, literal bankruptcy, and sexisim. Result? Lost election. Clinton was Weak In Military Potential. Worse, instead of attacking *Trump* she attacked his *supporters.* How could she have been so stupid? Attacking Trump's supporters guarantied they would never vote for her and would likely vote for him. Motivating your opponent's base is a stupid electoral move. Clinton did exactly that by calling Trump's supporters a "basket of deplorables".

The election was Hillary's to lose and she blew it by claiming to "put a lot of coal company's out of business", losing Pennsylvania and West Virginia, *states she could have won*, in a single sentence. She lost the Indian vote by claiming Trump was "off the reservation", which is an insult in Indian country: Members of the native nations have every right to be on or off the reservation, pilgrim. She furthermore referred most infamously to Trump's voters as "a basket of deplorables", which energized her opponent's base, motivating them to campaign and get out and vote themselves, and made it much less likely that she might have split off some of Trump's voters and gotten them to vote for her instead. American people generally don't like elitist know-it-alls: even educated Americans are anti-intellectual, self proclaimed pragmatists - which is code for cynical opportunist – hi Hillary! American elites and non-elites are also greedy economic inegalitarians: they *all* want to get rich and they almost all think the rich *deserve* to be rich. Elites and non-elites in the USA are also alike in that they are internally split as to whether the poor deserve poverty. Perhaps even more rich people think the poor deserve to be poor than the poor in the USA however across the board the majority Americans indeed believe the poor *deserve* to be poor. This is the flip-side of dishwasher-to-millionnaire Horatio Alger self-reliance: it's *your* fault if you are fucked, not the system. Of course this isn't always or perhaps even usually the case. So what?

For all these reasons, Clinton lost the election and Americans true to form will say she *deserved* to lose: I might agree. Meanwhile, Trump only insulted people *who could not vote for him* anyway: Mexicans and illegal immigrants. He only attacked political opponents, not their supporters or the voters. Never once did Trump insult Clinton's voters: I don't believe Clinton ever apologized to Indians, Black "Super Predators", or "Deplorables" or out of work coal miners. Even where Trump attacked specific individuals such as McCain, they still bent over to back him into office. So, despite his many flaws, Trump was elected. Trump won because he knows how to mobilize his base, split his opponents, due to the class structure of the United States and because he is a more personable public speaker and indeed a showman. He knew how to present himself as a popular well-liked powerful person to the majority of voters in swing states and so he won.

Trump represents the white majority of the United States, primarily, and secondarily the black people born in the United States and perhaps also Indians. Trump is not racist or anti-semitic or homophobic. He is at worst, a nativist, a nicer Ann Coulter. He is not a totalitarian, authoritarian, or white supremacist. In a sense, Trump is in fact the continuation of the integration of the black nation into the mainstream of the United States. So of course he would attack Elizabeth Warren's unjustified and disproven claim of Indian ancestry. How dare she claim to be something she isn't! You know who else Trump won? The Amish. Every vote counts. Clinton thought it was all about the elites. Trump didn't. So she lost.

Although most Hispanic people did not vote for trump because of his claimed anti-immigration views - some did, and more abstained from voting. Trump kept the disaffected whites and blacks united and got out their vote. Thus, he had the numbers to win the presidency of the United States. Clinton was unable to split Trumps "zebra" base most evidently in Michigan, a state which she could have won and which Democrats traditionally do win. It was Clinton's election to lose and she blew it by focusing on elites in Brooklyn at rather than getting out the vote, due to a certain repulsive elitist arrogance. Her last minute decision to focus her final attentions on winning a clear majority of voters in states she was certain to win anyway so as to claim a mandate was also an error. Clinton ought better to have focused her final energies on winning the swing states she lost rather than on securing a Pyrrhic mandate. She lost the election in West Virginia, Pennsylvania, Ohio, Michigan, and Wisconsin - not Brooklyn. Trump won the election in Detroit *and Michael Moore told you he would.*

Most of the elites dislike trump: this is partly due to class reasons. Trump says all sorts of rude things, what a fucking shame. But that's unacceptable to the globalizing elite even though swearing like a sailor is perfectly ok in the minds of non-elites. *Of course rich white men grab women by the pussy and if you're rich they really DO let you get away with it!* That might be a terrible truth, it's certainly roughly stated, but it's a fact: wealth and power are generally sexually attractive to most people. Furthermore, dominant behavior by men is usually considered sexy by the majority of women.

The globalizers argue that free trade and free movement of workers lead to greater productivity, greater wealth, and fewer wars. By and large the globalizing elite is right about that, by and large. However, that does not mean there are no losers in globalization: not just relative losers who get less rich more slowly but actual absolute losers who are impoverished as their high paying union jobs have almost entirely disappeared in a giant sucking sound of open borders and union busting. These disaffected people, the losers or self-perceived losers of globalization, are Trump's base. They live in the above mentioned swing states. They go to Walmart and buy cheap goods from China but are unable to make the connection that Walmart is cheap because the wages in China are low. They no longer have jobs in steel mills or car factories because their wages were too high. Their unions were broken by Reagan. Since wages in the developing world are half *or less* (usually much less) than those in the global core, outsourcing blue collar jobs will continue. Trump obviously knows this. Some people, a minority, will not be able to adjust to a knowledge economy: we can't all be microbiologists, some people are stupid and others prefer working with our hands. The problem is, there are no high paying hand-work jobs in the USA other than "surgeon", a monopoly profession that requires brains and hand-work. Trump's base is the disaffected and unlearned losers of globalization in the United States, which is more or less why you can see his base as proto-fascist.

B. Is Trump a New Hitler? Triumph of the Swill

As I predicted during the campaign, both Hilary Clinton and Donald Trump emerged as presidential nominees. The machinations of the of the republican party will be increasingly intriguing. Much like a rat which has eaten a poison pill, the republican party will writhe and twist, toss and turn, trying to shake off a parasite which exists only in its own mind, unaware of the true cause of its demise: poisoned from within, not flea-bites from without. For decades, repulsive republicans carefully cultivated a sophisticated passive racism, built a police state, scapegoated blacks and immigrants, all while pandering to corrupt financial interests from silverado S&L to the bankers' bail-out. President Trump embodies all of that: the Republican party sowed the wind of racism and crony corruption and now must reap the whirl-wind. The chickens have finally come home to roost. President Donald Trump, crowing like a cock will destroy the Republican party from within, the logical end-game for policies which started with Willy Horton and have continued ever since. There is nothing the Republicans or anyone else can do about it at this point short of assassinating Trump. That is a nuclear option I expect no one to use, since he who kills may in turn be killed and most people are unwilling to use violence and/or are fearful of the consequences of using violence. Furthermore, I will show here that there is no particular reason to murder Trump. If his actions are so terrible as I fear he will simply be indicted, impeached, and ultimately removed from office. He is probably already doomed to being a one-term president. So, the republicans elected a mild version of Hitler a possible traitor, with murky finances. Their party's ideology is destroyed from within and their party's outward credibility is ruined. If the Republican party splinters this will be the ultimate reason why.

Many people like to compare Trump to Hitler. Is Trump a fascist, a new Hitler? People make the comparison because Trump's political base is involuted and capable of violence. However, people who compare Hitler and Trump generally don't know enough German history to do so competently to discern the similarities and the divergences.

There is a shred of truth to the comparison of Trump with Hitler, but just a shred. While there are some few similarities, there are also many differences. Despite this, many people compare Trump to Hitler. For my part, I have lived and worked in Germany for many years and know U.S. and German history well. Consequently I will talk about the Hitler-Trump comparison. That comparison is frankly unfair to Trump.

Spoiler alert: Trump is more like Ponzi than Hitler: it is Putin, not Trump, who is most like Hitler.

Hitler was populist. So is Trump. Hitler faced governmental paralysis worse than Washington gridlock and filibusters: Weimar Germany was a basket case of unstable short-lived governments incapable of governing, mass unemployment, and hyper-inflation.

Hitler came to power at the head of a street-fighting populist movement, literally engaged in running gun battles in the streets and violent demonstrations with communist revolutionaries. Trump might be willing to engage in street-fighting tactics, if necessary - but that won't be necessary and has not and likely will not occur. Unlike Germany in the 1930s, the USA today has not been crippled by a global war, just the opposite. The limited Weimarization in the USA - gridlock filibusters - is not nearly as deep as the political paralysis which was the defining characteristic of the Weimar republic in Germany, which featured governments incapable of governing, and unable or unwilling to rein in the Communist-Freikorps-Nazi street battles and political criminality. Furthermore, U.S. "Weimarization" occurs before the background of the world's largest economy. The U.S remains a raw materials superpower and its unproductive services sectors are administers of a global economy. That is totally unlike Weimar Germany, where the economy was utterly ruined: bankrupted by war reparations, facing hyper-inflation, the German economy in the 1930s was much much worse than Michigan's today. Even intelligent hard-working people had no economic chance in late Weimar Germany, thanks to hyper-inflation and war reparations payments, unlike the contemporary USA.

The U.S. industrial base today could be rebuilt quickly simply by cutting minimum wages in half. Germany required threatening a world war to rebuild it's industry, then got it, and has regretted it ever since.

The fact is, the United States could function as an autarchic economy, doing quite well for itself even without Chinese inputs. The converse is not true. The Chinese economy would quickly collapse without U.S. markets to sell to, U.S. raw materials to purchase, and U.S. knowledge to exploit. This reality on the one hand enables Trump to get away with crass bellicosity. It also constrains China to realistic policies: I do not expect China will act like Putin, especially seeing where Putinism has led the Russian economy. In any case, the base of mass discontent and governmental paralysis which brought Hitler to power just is not there for Trump: a majority of American's are not in fact unemployed or even disaffected. There is no critical mass of radicals or even people who could be radicalized for Trump to impose a dictatorship and wage wars of conquest. Yet, Trump was shrewd enough to note a disaffected U.S. base in swing states actual or potential, exploited it, and so he won: simple as that. He quite capably targeted an audience ignored by the dominant ideology of both parties, winning thereby the swing states and thus the election. If anything makes him unimpeachable it is that fact: impeachment would confirm to his mass base that the system is corrupt and does not serve its interest, and then the Michigan militias would wind up acting like the Freikorps. But if they do they will get quickly crushed like the bonus army was. Even in the worst case Trump will not implement an American dictatorship.

We have elections so we do not have wars. Elections are a kind of war, complete with campaigns and strategy, a war of ideas waged with ballots instead of bullets. Thus, faction is ever a risk of democracy, but Federalist 10 teaches how to cure democracy of fractious factionalism.

Trump won because he is intelligent and a tough-talker, and that appeals to a majority of U.S. people. He is well aware his anti-immigrant stance is impossible in practice and has already spoken publicly of "self-deportation", which is unrealistic. Personally speaking, I have never self-deported

and never knew anyone who did. Trump's presidency is not
the isolationist fear-trade anti-immigrant Hitlerian hate-fest
that the global governing elite rightly fear and his opponents
tout. Their fears, though not entirely unjustified, have so far
proven inaccurate. Trump does however know how to
arbitrage and leverage the fears of the disaffected while
implementing policies the elite favors. Trump simply knows
how to play a mass base and also knows which policies do
or do not work. Trump convinced the suit-and-tie crowd, the
governing elites, that "the fix is in" and that all his bluster is
bluff is "all bark no bite". Thus, he did not face a united
opposition by the global governing elite and won the
election.

Can he do the same with his unsavory friends linked to the
Russian mafia? I sure hope not! I hope President Trump
throws all the U.S. criminals them under the bus. Every Last
One.

This is not to say that Trump is not a fraud. Trump ran a
"university" which was investigated for criminal fraud. That
is just one of the black marks on his record. Trump
furthermore managed to borrow millions of dollars in loans
only to go bankrupt, and this more than once. After that he
could only get loans and investments from other desperate
white people: Russian criminals, the "thieves of in the law",
the Russian state-mafia combo.

Really, all Clinton had to do to win was to simply point out
Trump lacks business acumen, is bad with business, is a
fraud: pointing out his mafia supporters would also have

been a good idea. She didn't: so she's a loser. How can someone be so stupid? One word. Yale.

If it's true it isn't a smear. If it's true it isn't libel or slander.

Clinton was not mean enough or disciplined enough or shrewd enough to spot the weaknesses in Trump's campaign or even meet his strategy, *which he announced during the campaign* to carry the industrial Midwest. Clinton also failed to press any of these points home with a passionate savage intensity. She lost similar infighting to Obama, undisputed leader of the black nation in the U.S.A., back in 2008. Obama could have played kingmaker in 2016, either solidifying Trump's base or splitting it. Whether he chose not to is a fine question: in fact however Obama did not adequately mobilize his black base to get out the vote for Clinton. Whether that is his fault is also a fine question, but the fact is black people did not turn out in the numbers they did for Obama when Clinton ran.

Clinton was electable. The Clinton's have certainly faced smear campaigns before. But they also seemed largely to immune to smears, "nothing burgers". Simply smearing Clinton would not have won the presidency for Trump, but in combination with other tactics smears certainly helped Trump's campaign, especially because Clinton never attacked Trump on his weakest points: Serial bankrupt, fraudster, with business ties to the Russian mafia and murky tax records – all of which are facts, which she failed to even try to press home. Maybe she had something to hide after all? Trump had no experience with political smear campaigns, so she probably would have out-smeared him had she only tried. Clinton failed to turn Trump's tax returns into "the birth certificate" issue that Obama so often faced. Just pointing out the facts: Donald Trump is a bankrupt business failure and a literal fraud, might have gotten Clinton elected despite her flaws - even without speculating to the voters what other scams, lies, frauds, or scandals are lurking in Donald Trump's closet, stuffed as it is with various Russians. Those other lurking scams lies and frauds are now leaking out and so Trump might faces the prospect of impeachment.

Clinton's foreign policy failures, Libya and Syria, unlike her political errors, were likely irrelevant to the election. Voter's don't care about foreign policies, just about winning wars, seeing their soldier-relatives home safely with medals and a fat paycheck. The economy was doing well. The election was hers to lose -- and she blew it. Obama is no longer King - but can be Kingmaker in 2020 with his (splinter?) democratic group "organizing for action".

1. Scapegoating and Militarism

Hitler and Trump both scapegoat, blaming weak groups for problems of the entire society. Hitler liked to blame Jews and Communists for everything. Unlike Hitler, Trump does not scapegoat Jewish people. Instead, like many republicans and some democrats, Trump scapegoats immigrants, Moslems, and foreigners. Trump unites people around hate and fear: so did Hitler. However, unlike Hitler, Trump does not have the military training or combat experience to lead a street-fighting coup d'état or win over the praetorians, actual or would-be. Trump's only military experience was attending prep school. Trump went to the so-called "New York Military Academy", a high-school, which in 2015 -- surprise surprise -- went bankrupt. After prep school, Donald Draft-Dodger went on to magically turn himself from 1A --most qualified for the draft -- into 4F: undraftable. People notice such things. So, the wannabe war-criminal, Donald Trump does not have the support of former military people. Mattis is there to serve *America*, not Trump. Dukakis is a great example about how people who actually serve or served in the military are not taken in by appearances and people who give lip-service to patriotism or deride military service. Dukakis rode a tank, and it did not make him look good in anyone's eyes. Trump insults tortured war veterans, and served in the U.S. military precisely never. Given the loudmouth's lack of real-world military experience or even training and his lack of military contacts dumbo will not be able to run a coup d'etat. As for Trump's desire to be war-criminal in chief? Please. Trump wants to torture more people. About that, the former head of the CIA already said:

'Bring your own damn bucket'.

Trump will not be able to lead any kind of coup: he has no contacts, no experience, no training.

2. A Broke Divided Nation?

Unlike Hitler, Trump does not face a broken, bankrupted nation, divided and ruined – though apparently he thinks he does. In other words, Trump is either out of touch with reality or prevaricating and grand-standing: the smart money picks /B/. Not only is the U.S.A. not broke and busted like Germany was in 1929 - America today *still* dominates the globe, despite all the errors of Bush, errors which Trump rightly reviles. The world's largest air force is still the U.S. Air force. The world's second largest air force is still the <u>U.S. Navy</u> (<u>NAVAIR</u>). So there is not in fact the mass-base for fascism or discontent which made Hitler possible. Trump plainly believes America is screwed up. Maybe marginally, maybe at the margins. But in general? No.

So, although Trump might scapegoat Jews for financial corruption (Madoff), treason (Pollard), and hypocritical dishonesty (Kristol), he hasn't so far, hardly surprising seeing as his daughter is a Jewish convert. For all his scapegoating of immigrants and Moslems, Trump's stage is not a bankrupted defeated country. He cannot credibly blame immigrants, Moslems, or Jews for the failures in the American Republic.

3. Political Paralysis & Gridlock (Weimarization)

Yet, America, like Germany in 1930, *is* factionalized and Weimarized into paralytic zero-sum dynastic factions. Federalist Number 10 warned us against exactly the polarization and factionalism which we see gripping *both* major parties, not only during primaries nor even during the campaign, but even after the election cycle is over we see zero sum politics polarized factionalism. Benjamin Franklin *also* warned us against polarization and faction: "A republic *if* you can keep it." The USA does face a real governance crisis, which explains the rise of Trump. Unfortunately, Trump is not yet able to resolve this crisis: Trump's ideas presented by critics as childish, are somewhat simplistic and underdeveloped. President Trump has identified some of the problems, but has not yet proposed workable solutions.

The United States, like Weimar Germany, faces gridlock, political paralysis and numerous cultural and economic challenges. However, it is not Germany, 1933. The economy is not bankrupted nor are millions unemployed nor does the USA face hyperinflation. However, the USA today, like Germany back then does face political paralysis. Still, the U.S. in 2016 is just "House of Cards" and not "Game of Thrones" – and like House of Cards, Trump's presidency may end in some variety of sex scandal...

Trump is trying to react against Weimar style gridlock, using nationalism. He might be able to rescue the republic from gridlock do-nothings despite corruption within his own faction. However, his populist base, though a necessary precondition for a real political breakthrough, is not in itself sufficient. An ultra-nationalist populist base coupled with ridiculous <u>foreign policy ideas that read like a cheap cracker-jack prize</u> results in no election and no reform. Great Wall of Mexico? Please. Torture-the-Planet? Self-destructive stupidity. Raise Tariffs? To bad Prince is no longer here to tell us that tonight we're gonna party like its 1929... For the supposed economic genius here's a flyby of 1929:

I don't think Trump is trying to provoke a stock market crash. However, real estate does not lose value in the face of a stock market crash. Short the futures market much?

Rather than provoking a 1929 style economic crash, world war, or coup d'état, Trump may only succeed in uniting the economic and political élites against him leading to impeachment. <u>Charles Koch</u> for example said that Clinton would make a decent president. Trump does of course have the support of some cultural élites, some Hollywood types. But his potential opponents will likely have more cultural backers, and not just those in Hollywood. What NEA grantee would expect help from Trump or have a message backing up Trump's line? How many sensitive compassionate people love Trump?

Meanwhile, the fact that <u>Trump is a bankrupt fraudster will increasingly become plain</u>. In sum: Trump is a fraud, a bankrupt, and probably unfit for the office of President of the United States.

Fraud is misrepresentation of a material fact inducing reliance and causing damage: the material facts? That Trump would lead and/or designed the course materials for a university; these representations clearly were false, Trump did not design or lead the courses, and the courses were not offered by a university. These fraudulent statements in turn obviously induced reliance, resulting damage in the form of paid tuition: Trump settled what was obviously an open and shut case.

Trump is baking like a chickenhawk in the sun, and is being set up for slow-roasting in a solar cooker!

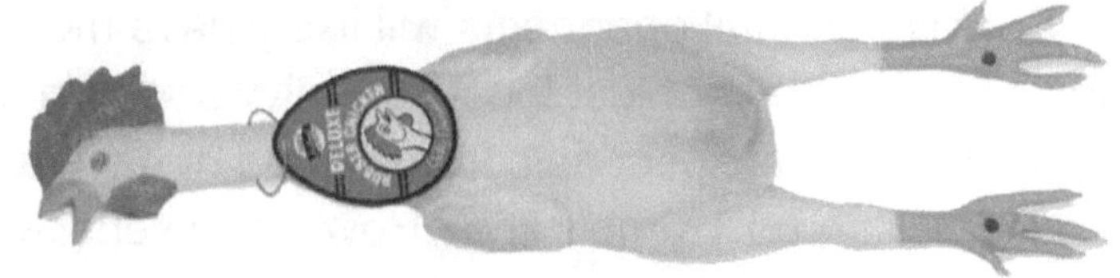

FOLLOW ME

"You First!" The War-Cry of every Chickenhawk!

C. IS TRUMP FIT TO BE THE PRESIDENT OF THE UNITED STATES?

1. From Draft Dodger to Commander in Chief
The transformation - or is it destruction? - of the Republican party by Trump can be traced back to the failure of the Republican party to self-discipline and exclude Trump based on his prior political acts which go against core republican values:

1) Trump dodged the draft. Militant patriotism is a core republican value.
2) Trump is a serial bankrupt. Fiscal responsibility and economic sanity are also core republican values.
3) Trump favors protectionism. Free trade was a consensus republican *and* democratic elite core value
4) Trump opposes immigration. Open immigration was a consensus republican *and* democratic elite core value.

Were there any doubt Trump is not so patriotic as most republicans might think, we need only recall his various *insults* to the U.S. Military. Trump won despite insulting and dishonoring McCain (who endorsed him anyway...), the handicapped, women, Mexicans, and advocating foolish policies like the Great Wall of Mexico and the Great Tariff Wall of China. Trump won because *Clinton was that bad*. Despite the basic contradictions Trump presents to core republican values he nonetheless rallied a a majority of the élites who really run this world behind his isolationist anti-globalization line. Why? Becaue he could, and did, deliver the votes in swing states and transformed democratic safe states into swing states carried by republicans.

Furthermore, the elites who support Trump are basically gambling Trump cannot or will not implement the sensationalist aspects of his foreign policy or are putting party above country, self-interest above national interest, or are simply self-serving opportunistic traitors.

Donald Trump believes war crimes are the way to win wars. While that appeals to at least 20% of the U.S., and possibly even to the majority, it is wrong. War crimes lose wars, ask Hitler. Speaking about General Pershing Trump said: "And he lined up the 50 people and they shot 49 of those 50 people, and he said to the 50th, you go back to your people and you tell them what happened -- and in 25 years there wasn't a problem". Untrue, but since when do bankrupt fraudsters care about the truth or insulting dead Generals?

EXTRACT OF REGISTRANT CLASSIFICATION RECORD

The following information concerning the Selective Service registrant named has been extracted from the Classification Record (SSS Form 102). Unless otherwise noted, all entries on this record are included. See reverse side for brief explanation of classification descriptions.

Name of registrant: DONALD J. TRUMP

Selective Service No.: 50 · 63 · 46 · 580   Date of Birth: JUNE 14, 1946

Classification Questionnaire: Date Mailed 6/24/64   Date Returned

Classification and Date of Mailing Notice:

1. Class 2·S   Date 7/28/64   5. Class 2·S   Date 1/16/68
2. Class 2·S   Date 12/14/65   6. Class 1·A   Date 7/9/68
3. Class 1·A   Date 11/22/66   7. Class 1·Y   Date 10/15/68
4. Class 2·S   Date 12/13/66   8. Class 4·F   Date 2/1/72

Armed Forces Physical Examination: Date(s): 12/15/66 ; 9/17/68   Results: DISQ

(Qual - Qualified; Acc - Accepted; NQ - Not Qualified; Rej - Rejected)

Entry on Active Duty or Civilian Work: Date:

Branch of Service (if indicated):

Mode of Entry: ☐ Inducted (IND)   ☐ Enlisted (ENL)
               ☐ Commissioned (COMM)   ☐ Ordered

Date of Separation from Active Duty or Civilian Work:

Entries from Remarks Column: Y XX

OTHER ENTRIES: Entered below are any entries (with the appropriate column headings) which appear on the original classification record and for which there is no fill-in space above:

TO: FRC USE ONLY

                                             Date Prepared: 4/28/11

                                             Prepared By:

Trump is a draft dodger: he got a draft deferment for a "medical" condition and magically dropped from 1A -- fit to fight -- to 4F which is about the last person who gets drafted. Who smells a rat? Is this change in recordation the result of bribery? Here is Trump's Draft Dodging, recorded for all to see:

Looking at these facts, one can logically conclude, unfortunately, that Trump is a hypocritical draft dodger, a bankrupt, a fraud, and thus unfit to be president. *Clinton pointed none of that out, which is why she lost.* Why didn't Clinton point out any of that? Either Clinton was incompetent or there were back room deals out of the public view or perhaps she was aiming to destroy the republican party, and miscalculated. Maybe Clinton really does have dirty laundry of her own? Probably Clinton expected Trump would tear apart the republican party from within, and lose the election. However, he won. Whether he will indeed tear apart the republican party remains to be seen.

Would-be war criminal Donald Trump who never served in the U.S. Military, which looks like draft-dodging to me appears unfit to be the Commander in Chief of the United States Army. Those of us who actually wore the uniform, served honorably, and defended the United States must stand up against this imposter. Army Field Manual FM 6-22 (FM22-100) "Military Leadership" specifically points out that the United States of America does not shoot prisoners of war (4-2), opposes torture (4-15) and does not undertake reprisal massacres (4-14). You know why? Because the United States fights to win, and killing prisoners is a great way to make your enemy fight to the death and not surrender. Torturing prisoners is a great way to make the enemy fight even harder. Hitler tried the sorts of tactics Trump advocates in Russia and you know what? Once Russia figured out what the Nazis were doing the Russians kicked the hell out of the nazis and won World War II. Trump's tactics would lose America's wars and get lots of people needlessly killed. He is unfit for the role of commander in chief of the greatest military force history has ever seen.

Clinton failed to call Trump a cowardly draft dodging bankrupt fraudster, so she lost. If she had half a brain and wanted to win the white house she would have called Trump a cowardly draft dodger who thinks the U.S. Army are a bunch of war criminals, the "swift boat" treatment. Hillary didn't swift boat Trump so now we have him. I think some military men would not follow him to the bathroom let alone the battlefield.

2. The Bankrupt President for Bankruptcy

Although the basic facts of fiscal and monetary policy are obvious to any well-educated person, Trump ignores them. Trump is willing to undermine U.S. credit worthiness. Trump is willing to default on U.S. debts. Why? Is there some greater reason, some pressing problem of the national interest which would justify defaulting on U.S. debt and plunging the world into another great recession with broad-ranging U.S. unemployment? A new world war? A catastrophe? Some justification for telling U.S. creditors "fuck you"? No.

Then why is Trump undermining the credit of the U.S.
Treasury bond and the U.S. dollar?
To support his personal political ambition, that's why.

Of course, as soon as Trump indicated he is willing to
cause a default on U.S. bonds idiotic apologists
immediately started sucking up. Some of Trump's ideas are
crazy smart: but others are scary stupid.

Consequently, Trump is meeting increasing opposition
within the Republican party. Republican leaders, tending to
be wealthy, and tending to want wealth, are well aware of
the realities of capital markets, and of the disaster debt
default would unleash. Yet, true to form, Trump doubled
down, a living example of the sunk costs fallacy and
escalation of commitment. People tend to remain

committed to their prior decisions even where those decisions are wrong because it is generally better to be decisive and persistent. There are exceptions and the ability to distinguish when one should accept their losses and move on as opposed to being stubborn as a mule. Trump even brags that he is "the king of debt". What a wonderful thing to be king of!

Who wants to be ruled by a king of debt? Certainly not the rich elites. Some of the policies Trump proposes, if implemented, would be catastrophically stupid.

Because some of Trump's proposed policies are stupid, and would be catastrophic for the United States the republican party will likely split, failing to unify behind Trump. The Republican party may splinter into two or more parties. Ryan looks to be the most likely leader either of a rump Republican party. Likely leaders of a republican/tea party/white nationalist splinter party are … Bannon. Whether the Republicans will split, become irrelevant, or transform into a de facto permanent ruling party has yet to be seen with certainty.

This campaign was ugly. The election was Hillary's to lose. She lost it. Trump consistently called Clinton, and I quote: "crooked", "mean", and "nasty". Clinton, in contrast, never called Trump a bankrupt stupid fraud. So she lost. Simple as that. However, that betides a fractured polity, the decline (and fall?) of civil discourse.

Is it also the harbinger of a mafia state?

3. Trump Clinton and Alinsky: The Mafia States of America?

Like I predicted at the time, Trump emerged as the nominee of the republican party and won the election. Among Republicans, Paul Ryan was the first (and not the only "insider" to refuse to support Trump and will likely be one of the first to turn against him if past performance is indicative of the future. Warren Buffet for his part indicated that he was not worried by trump. Thus, Clinton treated Trump gently, with "kid gloves", which was obviously a mistake. Sanders was less civil, but was constrained by his collegiate supporters to roar like the cowardly lion.

The democratic primary ended with Bernie Sanders losing slowly and painfully to Clinton with no overt sparring over the role of Sanders after the election. Thus it is likely that mainstream democrats will have to make some sort of deal with Sanders if they are to unite the democratic party for 2020.

Clinton correctly pointed out the hole that Trump has dug himself into, and she should have kept doing that if she wanted to win the presidency. Really, all she had do was to have applied one of Alinsky's rules for radicals: hold your opponent to your opponent's own rules, i.e. make your opponent keep his word -- because he can't. Clinton could have merely reposted, reblogged, restated, reiterated all the horrible things Trump said and might have won thereby. Clinton should have called Trump a bankrupt and a fraud, *but she didn't.* Clinton was far too measured and reserved in her own statements, leaving the mud slinging to her loyalists, the <u>Clintonistas</u>. Her <u>mudslingers-by-proxy</u> were remarkably quiet and ineffective.

In sum, the 2016's campaign was bitter and dirty. It was an election led by the élites on one side, fighting for an open world order with free trade: the liberal internationalists. Opposing them, the non-elites led by their champion strongman Vladimir Trump (not a typo). Those non-elites are reactionary and fearful, and understandably so, given their personal and economic background. Non-elites are excluded from power and impoverished and often exhibit involuted or even unintelligent thinking. Trump talks isolationism and non-interventionism. So there might at first be fewer wars if Trump wins - at first. However, his anti-immigrant and anti free-trade line will, if implemented, result in a global recession. If Trump's ideas against free-trade and immigration are taken up a global recession and poverty will result. Then, Trump will only be able to give his constitutents "good jobs" in the military. In that case, once Trump has all those gun-loving desperate poor white people in uniform he will have to do something with them -- after all he will be paying them good money. So, as a result of the trade wars and recessions which he would preside over Trump will inevitably send the whiter brighter(?) U.S. military overseas to enforce Trump's world-order: this looks like **a global protection racket**, the mafia writ large. To the cynics:

Trump is running a three-punch mafia strategy.

Step one, **the con-game** -- con the voters. Convince voters and donors that Trump is not a bankrupt fraudster but instead is a brilliant negotiater. President Trump has accomplished this, having won the election, because Clinton was either too timid to say relentlessly two words: bankrupt fraudster.

Step two: **the protection racket**. Extract payments from U.S. allies. Countries which don't do what the U.S. wants will be made to pay, one way or the other. President Trump is trying to do this currently.

Step three: **the <u>bust-out</u>**. Having run up as much debt as possible, which will be necessary since Trump's economic policies, if taken up, will cause a global recession. **<u>Trump will</u>** then <u>default</u> on U.S. foreign debt obligations. <u>Buffet will wind up opposing Trump</u>, but whether that will be too late is yet to be seen.

His daughter's really hot though so it's all good, rite?

Obviously President Trump has not yet bankrupted the USA, but if he does that will unleash a global recession and many wars. Consequently, Trump's foreign policy for the Mafia States of America would then impose neo-colonialism on those parts of the world which are unable to resist.

Putin's Russia will be able to resist Trump, and so Trump and Putin will fall out of each others' favor. Putin probably already knows this, and Trump will figure it out sooner rather than later - there is no honor among thieves. Trump will talk neo-isolationism, live-and-let-live, flexibility, unpredictability. But in the end Trump will probably, whether by choice or constraint, preside over more interventionism, to the detriment of the republic.

Unlike Clinton and Obama, so far as I have seen Trump is unaware of or untrained by Alinskyites. Alinsky was literally a friend of various mafia. Clinton wrote her undergraduate thesis on Alinsky.

To understand the rise of Clinton and conflicts with Putin, conflicts which would ultimately be even worse were Trump elected, we need to look back at Saul Alinsky. Alinsky was a Russian Jewish left wing activist, probably a crypto-communist, certainly a socialist. He may well have been aware of Okhrana methods such as disinformation, provocation, masking (дезинформация, провокация, маскировка). While these might not be Trump's methods they certainly are the methods of the SRV and FSB, handlers of Manafort, Trump's indicted former campaign manager. Even if Alinsky was unaware of these methods, he somehow managed to come up with activist methods that are fairly comparable to the methods used by the USSR, though perhaps more honest. Knowing this, it should come as no surprise that Russia Today claims that the U.S. is using Alinskyite methods in Ukraine. Meanwhile, the <u>Wall Street Journal claims Putin is using Alinskyite methods</u> in Ukraine.

<u>What if they are both right?</u>

D. Explaining *2016* from Intra and Inter Party Politics

My best guess as to Clinton's strategy in 2016 was that she was aiming to destroy the republican party by splintering it by fostering unelectable candidates and candidates who would rip the GOP apart from within. How better to explain her errors? While Clinton could not directly influence the GOP nomination, she could, and in my opinion did, influence the nomination indirectly in her reactions and perhaps also through the reactions of Obama, which exacerbated the problems and conflicts within the republican party. If that hypothesis is correct then Clinton's goal was to sow chaos and confusion as well as dissent among republican ranks, as reflected in the speculation about a "coalition" among anti-Trump candidates at the republican convention to prevent the nomination of Trump by the Republican party as that party's candidate for President of the United States. Their objective, of course, was to create conditions for a "brokered" politico convention, wherein the Republican party élite would select a candidate at the convention through typical "horse-trading" – delegitimating the candidate so selected in democratic terms, and thus making him less likely to be elected and if elected less able to govern effectively. Trump rightly pointed out that the efforts to mount a convention challenge against him as collusion, evidence of a certain anti-democratic élite corruption within the republican party, and also evidence of his rivals' weakness. Consequently, Trump secured the nomination despite any collusion among the other candidates. His tactics were apt *both* during the nomination *and* during the general election and so people who dismiss Trump as stupid or crazy are wrong. You might disagree with his politics, but his tactics and strategy, even if disagreeable to some (especially his enemies) – worked! **Clinton was able to exploit the splits withing the republican party to influence who was chosen by the republicans but to her surprise lost to the candidate she indirectly favored in the nomination process.**

Dream or nightmare?

The hard question Clinton faced wasn't "can Clinton influence the republican selection process so as to choose her rival". The question she faced was *which* republican rival would be *more* easily defeated in the general election. Probably her best bet to both 1) destroy the republicans and 2) win the general election would have been to indirectly favor Cruz. However, Cruz would have been much less likely to destroy the republican party from within, which Trump has already done and Trump *looked* unelectable to almost everyone, especially on the left, except for me and Michael Moore. While Clinton might have lost against Cruz if he were to run unchallenged that is a maybe: Cruz was young, inexperienced, and Canadian. If Clinton had faced Cruz I expect she would have won due to greater experience and lots of political debts owed to her. But the republican party would have been much less fragmented and scandalized than it is currently.

In the end, the entire élite sector will probably finally rally against Trump because **Trump says ridiculous things - and often means them.**

Trump is like a clown in that 1) the U.S. is an immigrant country and needs immigrants a) to grow even richer b) to compete with China. America is a giant immigrant magnet and Trump's clownish anti-immigrant antics really only appeal to white America - which is now only about 60% of the U.S. population. Moreover, he only appeals to the disaffected and ultra-nationalists. Trump does not appeal to the white economic *or* cultural élites; no brains, no money. At best, his anti-immigrant policies are stupid prejudice: at worst, they are conscious sabotage of U.S. power to benefit his Russian friends.

Trump is *also* like a clown in that he believes that the U.S. can and should torture people. He is wrong, for the same reason Hitler was wrong on that point. The military will increasingly see that and increasingly rally against him.

How else is Trump like a clown? Well, a <u>fraudulent "university"</u>, a <u>string of bankruptcies</u>, these are not the marks of an economic genius. Trump is a bankrupt, a fraudster, and thus unfit for the office of President of the United States. Disagree? Sue me for defamation.

All the whining about corruption sleaze deception etc. regarding Clinton is just that: whining. In politics people make apparently inconsistent statements and positions in order to win an election. Clinton is no more, and possibly less corrupt than Trump.

II. Trump's Foreign Policy – Realist Economic Nationalism

"My goal is to establish a foreign policy that will endure for several generations. That's why I also look and have to look for talented experts with approaches and practical ideas, rather than surrounding myself with those who have perfect résumés but very little to brag about except responsibility for a long history of failed policies and continued losses at war. We have to look to new people." -Donald Trump

Trump's speech on foreign policy during the campaign was surprisingly cogent, despite his foreign policy inexperience. Trump rightly attacked Clinton's disastrous foreign policy during the last two years of her tenure as Secretary of State, specifically her ham-handed interventions in Syria and Libya the so-called "Arab Spring". However, the basic fact is the U.S. presidential election is never decided on foreign policy issues. George Bush senior, who presided over a brilliant foreign policy, learned that the hard way. "All politics is local" is a tried-and-true famous adage, and basically accurate. Foreign policy is no decisive campaign issue because the matters involved are outside ordinary people's experiences or interests. Most people do not know foreign languages, foreign history, or even geography. This is why countries have élites in foreign policy, who are expert in those fields. I happen to be such a person, though I am obviously not affiliated with any government or political campaign, being agnostic about such issues. Clinton's incoherent ineffective and deadly interventions in Syria and Libya were failures. However, that issue did not decide the election.

Like his voter-base, Trump's own ideas about foreign policy are simplistic, under-developed. Because foreign policy does not decide elections Trump did not need to think about foreign policy until after the election: at which point he should have done whatever the experts tell him to do. He has not however even filled all open high-level offices in the State Department, and thus has no high level advisers from whom to take expert advice. The results, which so far including outsourcing U.S. Foreign policy in the middle-east to Russia, will become increasingly obviously disastrous.

Unlike Trump, Clinton has foreign policy experience. Unfortunately, like Trump, she lacks foreign policy expertise, so her foreign policies proved in practice to be disasters. Does anyone really regard Libya or Syria as examples of success? The so-called Arab spring was a tragic joke, a deadly failed experiment which cost countless lives of ordinary Arabs. Clinton, Secretary of State, lacked any personal foreign policy expertise. Clinton's political ambit started as a legal aid and community organizer. She was never at CIA or State and seems rather …
monolingual. Lacking her own expertise, Clinton blindly tried to apply neoconservative regime change theory to Libya, Syria, Bahrain, Egypt in short anywhere in the Middle East, continuing the same republican policies which

obviously failed in Iraq. The results were disastrous: possibly less disastrous than out-sourcing U.S. Foreign policy in the middle east to Russia, but only arguably.

Clinton was a proven disaster in foreign policy. Yet, Trump's foreign policy may prove to be even worse than Clinton's, depending on what happens with the U.S. alliances such as NATO, US trade agreements such as NAFTA, and how much U.S. foreign policy is handed over to Russia.

Trump beat Clinton despite insulting and dishonoring McCain (who endorsed him anyway), the handicapped, women, Mexicans, and advocating foolish policies like the Great Wall of Mexico and the Great Tariff Wall of China: Clinton was that bad. In the end Trump rallied a a majority of the élites who really run this world behind his isolationist anti-globalization line. Probably the elites who support Trump believe he cannot or will not implement the sensationalist aspects of his foreign policy.

A. Trump's National Security Strategy:
1. Neo-Realism

At the same time as he is neo-isolationist, Trump claims to be a foreign-policy realist. Realists like Trump believe that nations and states are rational actors, maximizing their national self-interest, and that the nation-state is the basic building block of international relations. That view is partly responsible for two world wars: balance-of-power politics, divide-and-rule, do not generate stability or peace, goals Trump wishes to obtain. States do in fact tend to pursue their national interest as articulated by their élites. However, states are no longer the sole international actor. International organizations such as the UN, the EU, NAFTA serve important roles, coordinating trade, protecting human rights, preventing wars, all of which leads to greater prosperity and fewer wars. Trump does not know anything about the theory or history of international organizations.

Trump's foreign policy can be quickly summarized as economic nationalism in trade policy, and ill-considered neo-isolationism in security policy. Trump does not have a deep understanding of foreign policy, because it is largely outside his experiences. He does not see that he is seeking to lead the global hegemon, and so requires support not only of his advisers in the military and foreign services, but also among the literally dozens of countries which are in formal alliances with the United States. Trump believes American isolation is possible, but it is not. This is not merely due to economic factors, but also political ones. The United States cannot economically walk away from the world, Trump's possible fantasies to the contrary.

2. Neo-Isolationism
It is rather obvious Trump opposes globalization. He said: "We will no longer surrender this country or its people to the false song of globalism. The nation-state remains the true foundation for happiness and harmony. I am skeptical of international unions that tie us up and bring America down".

If that wasn't clear enough Trump also said:
"Instead of trying to spread universal values that not everybody shares or wants, we should understand that strengthening and promoting Western civilization and its

accomplishments will do more to inspire positive reforms around the world than military interventions."

Well, on the up-side, fewer wars, at least in the short run. On the down-side, no human rights. Once again, Trump throws minorities under the bus.

The opposite of globalization is isolationism. Trump is basically an isolationist.

The problem with isolationism is that it has been tried, and failed, causing two global wars. If the U.S. simply ignored the rest of the world that would create much instability, to the detriment of U.S. security and U.S. businesses. Even a quick reading of the history of the causes of the world wars shows that U.S. isolationism was one of the key causes of two world wars. No foreign country knew what U.S. policy would be in the event of war. Consequently, foreign countries were unable to structure their diplomatic arrangements appropriately. The result was two world wars. Trump thinks the President's foreign policy should be unpredictable, and apparently does not see that predictability is generally desirable to prevent and resolve conflicts and thus in the interest of the Unite States in maintaining a stable world order under U.S. auspices.

"The great wall of Mexico" is another example of how Trump's foreign policy is neo-isolationist. Trump's policies are self-consistent and organized around "America first". However, many of his foreign policy proposals are simplistic and would be disastrous if put into practice. In the real world the United States needs immigrants. The social security system was built on the presumption that people would live till about 60 and have about 4 children. Meanwhile, people now live to be about 80 or even more, and had only two children. The social security system is in that sense a ponzi scheme and it was built to co-opt potential troublemakers and lock-in the American worker in the run-up to World War II. Social security, without immigrants, is likely fiscally unsustainable. Immigrants are productive workers and taxpayers. All those people Trump would expel or ban from entry would be lost productivity for the United States and probably would hate and resent the United States. Who likes being kicked out like trash? Trump simply does not understand that the global economy is deeply interconnected. The neo-isolationism he advocates would be impossible and disastrous in practice.

3. Trump's Rejects Unilateralism
Trump also said:

"Finally, I will work with our allies to reinvigorate Western values and institutions. Instead of trying to spread universal values that not everybody shares or wants, we should understand that strengthening and promoting Western civilization and its accomplishments will do more to inspire positive reforms around the world than military interventions."

Trump made other similar clear statements about his views on the use of force, statements which I take seriously, and which you, dear reader, might also consider seriously.

"I will never sent our finest into battle unless necessary, and I mean absolutely necessary, and will

only do so if we have a plan for victory with a capital V."

"I will not hesitate to deploy military force when there is no alternative. But if America fights, it must only fight to win."

"The world must know that we do not go abroad in search of enemies, that we are always happy when old enemies become friends and when old friends become allies, that's what we want. We want them to be our allies.
... we want to bring peace to the world."

Trump seems smart enough to know he lacks the expertise he needs to run U.S. foreign policy, even though he has clear ideas about the direction that he wants U.S. foreign policy to go. He said: "My goal is to establish a foreign policy that will endure for several generations. That's why I also look and have to look for talented experts with approaches and practical ideas" Unfortuntely however, Trump has not in fact even appointed, let alone listened to, the foreign policy experts which he needs to effectively rule. This alone likely dooms him to a one-term presidency.

4. Trump Rejects Neoconservatism

人 的正确思想是从哪里来的？

"Where do correct ideas come from? Do they drop from the skies? No. Are they innate in the mind? No. They come from social practice, and from it alone; they come from three kinds of social practice, the struggle for production, the class struggle and scientific experiment."

— *Mao Zedong*

Although Trump is wrong to oppose globalization he is right to oppose neoconservatism. He evidently fails to distinguish those two things from each other. Consequently, he "throws the baby out with the bathwater". Isolationists and neoconservatives, though disagreeing with each other on many issues, are both incorrect, and in different ways.

Regarding neconservatism, Trump correctly opposes "nation building", an incoherent policy, generally used as a code-word for corruption of one variety or other. Trump, in his own words, wants to "defeat terrorists and promote regional stability, not radical change".

Unlike neocons, Trump is not planning to bring the world war after war with no end in sight. He said: "unlike other candidates for the presidency, war and aggression will not be my first instinct. You cannot have a foreign policy without diplomacy. A superpower understands that caution and restraint are really truly signs of strength. Although not in government service, I was totally against the war in Iraq, very proudly, saying for many years that it would destabilize the Middle East." Here, recall please, that when she was Senator Clinton voted in favor of the war in Iraq. Iraq, Libya, Syria, "Arab Spring" - all foreign policy failures, and all can be rightly attributed to Clinton. She simply should never have listened to neoconservatives, no matter how "well connected" or "well informed" they claimed to be.

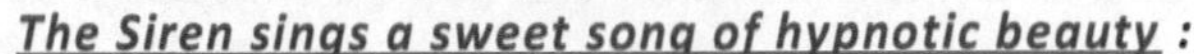

The Siren sings a sweet song of hypnotic beauty :

but lures sailors to their doom.

Whether implemented by democrats (Obama, Clinton) or republicans (Bush), neoconservative regime change fails to replace dictatorships with peaceful productive democracies that respect human rights. Trump recognized that, pushed that issue, and thus won the anti-war vote. Even neo-isolationism looked better than *another* decade *or more* of endless *avoidable* wars in the middle east. "Arab Spring" was wars *of choice.* No one *made* the USA encourage violent rebellion and civil war in Syria and the Syrian government, like Saddam Hussein, had not much if anything to do with Islamic extremist terrorism. Neoconservatives are more interested in draining the U.S. treasury and in sowing chaos and conflict in the Arab world, divide-and-rule, than in articulating or defending the interests of the United States. Moreover, neocons are fundamentally dishonest. Please read Leo Strauss yourself in case you don't believe me. Clinton voted in favor of the neocon's gulf war, and went on to get the U.S. Ambassador to Libya killed, not to mention thousands of Libyans and tens of thousands of Syrians, plus a few other U.S. citizen who prefer to remains nameless. All these people who died at Clinton's behest, victims of Clinton's policies. Clinton went to Yale, is not poor, and has no excuse for her failures. Moreover, she used her own unsecured personal email server for State Department work, and her server was very probably penetrated by foreign intelligence services.

Neoconservative Regime Change Theory", "Clash of Civilizations", and "Unrestricted warfare", are foolish wrong ideas - with deadly consequences for the world's poorest people, dooming nations and generations to avoidable conflicts. This fact explains why Trump rejects neoconservatism, even though his daughter converted to Judaism.

War is a disaster, but it is a man-made disaster. **We study war in order to prevent it.** All responsible intelligent people interested in international relations should understand those poisonous ideas and reject them - because they are wrong and have deadly consequences.

B. Trump's Trade Policy: "America First"

Trump's trade policy, unlike his national security strategy, if implemented will prove disastrous. Trump essentially opposes multilateral globalizing institutionalized free trade regimes such as NAFTA. Trump does not understand that free trade arrangements like NAFTA generate prosperity through trade and foster peace through prosperity and interdependence. Trump believes that the United States can unilaterally impose massive tariffs on China and place the costs of a big border wall on Mexico. The problem with massive unilateral tariffs is that they lead to trade wars impoverishing the U.S., China, and any other country so stupid as to get into the trade-war. Trump says "China respects strength". In fact, no. China respects *intelligence*. Chinese culture is more intellectual and less militaristic than Trump seems to think.

The desirable alternative to war is trade: voluntary trade is a positive-sum game. Each trading party benefits from the trade, otherwise they would not exchange their goods or make capital investments. Moreover, trade generates prosperity, which makes war less likely. Similarly, the mutual dependence trade brings makes war less likely.

Thus, it is much likelier that China and the USA will trade peacefully, on whatever terms, than that they go to war.

In an interview with the Wall Street Journal Chinese Finance Minister Lou Jiwei said some things about Donald Trump. Naturally, the election of Trump as the President had China quite concerned.

Alinsky in his "Rules for Radicals" rightly recommended to "fractionate" issues, to treat each issue separately, so as to defuse conflict, so to speak. I agree with Alinsky on fractionating issues, to better resolve conflict. According to dialectical materialism issues of peaceful trade and military security are qualitatively different. One represents a relative contradiction, the other an absolute one.

In <u>On Contradiction,</u> Mao describes absolute contradictions as contradictions between polar opposites. To Mao, in a case of absolute contradiction no compromise is possible. Mao then describes relative contradictions, and distinguishes them from absolute contradiction. In relative contradiction, the opposing tendencies are instances on a continuum and are only relatively opposed. In cases of relative contradiction compromise is possible, according to Mao. Contradictions over trade are generally relative contradictions, not absolute contradictions. Contradictions over defence and security, where they exist, tend to be absolute. Thus, it is correct to treat trade issues separately from security issues. Mao also identified the principal contradiction as the place where the Chinese Communist Party should place it's main efforts: Premier Xi has, if I understand, identified environmental pollution as the principal contradiction facing China, a realistic and hopeful sign that China will continue to clean up its own environment so as to improve the lives and particularly the health of ordinary Chinese people.

Because China is a single party people's dictatorship it's domestic political processes are to a certain extent inscrutable and also inaccessible to outsiders. This is why I rarely talk about Chinese domestic politics, even though I understand Marxism quite deeply.

Just as it may be difficult for the U.S. diplomats to always understand the inner workings of the Chinese Communist Party, so also it may be difficult for Chinese people, even at the ministerial level, to understand fine points about the internal political workings of the United States.

First, the United States does not have a formal party-political-system, unlike the People's Republic of China or Germany for that matter. Yet, de facto, as matter of fact, and not law, that is not de jure, the U.S. operates as a two-party system. Furthermore, this system implements the will of what Marx called the bourgeoisie: the global governing elite of wealthy educated people. Many of those elites are just as disgusted at the idea of a Trump presidency as anyone in China might be.

If the translation of the Chinese Minister's statements is correct the Minister considers trump "irrational". That goes a bit too far. I do not regard trump as insane. He is probably megalomaniacal, but he is also intelligent, logical. However, Trump is somewhat irresponsible and extreme in his statements, as any nationalist leader is. Trump is a blow-hard, and that is often part of being a politician. Of course, to the PRC, a Trump Presidency would look like Abe's tenure in office, and I do not mean Lincoln. I do not believe that Trump would be as extreme as Abe. I could be wrong and can well understand the concern of the globalising governing elites about his candidacy. For those seeking parallels, Trump is America's version of Umberto Bossi.

The Chinese Finance Minister said wise things, like this: "Our economic cycles are intertwined". As I pointed out earlier, one of the objectives of global liberalism is to integrate the developing world economies into a global economy to help grow their economy and make war less likely due to greater prosperity and interdependence. Trump, though a loud-mouth, knows that the U.S. is in an intertwined global economy and could never in practice implement half the nonsense he spouts. The global governing elites in the English speaking world know he could not implement his neo-isolationism, and the shrewder ones know that he knows it too: "self-deportation" is terribly funny. Is his base dumb enough to believe it? Maybe! It is for this reason, among others, inapt to compare Trump to Hitler, as some have done. Trump, like the global governing elite, knows that the U.S. needs immigrants and the majority of U.S. citizens are pro-immigration. The anti-immigrant crowd is vocal, motivated, and wrong. When Trump talks about starting a trade-war against China by raising tariffs the entire U.S. foreign policy community, including all of the academics, would just say no. No man, even a President, can implement a policy alone.

"People say my wall idea is crazy. China built a wall, and guess how many Mexicans they have?"

Politics is no joking matter!

Donald J Trump
Yesterday at 6:49 AM · 🌐

People say my wall idea is crazy. China built a wall, and guess how many Mexicans they have.

Checkmate.

Unless no one takes you seriously...

The error Trump faces is failing to win over the global governing elites, because he is genuinely against much of their line. When he talks about corruption within the republican party he does not mean bribery, whispering campaigns, extortion, abduction, financial fraud, or similar mafia problems. I do take his bringing the topic of corruption up as evidence that other than bankruptcy his own financial operations were on the up-and-up, a presumption about which I could well be wrong. But if Trump were a mafia contractor then he would not be likely to raise the topic of organized crime. Furthermore, the United States largely killed and imprisoned its domestic mafia back in the 1990s. Legalizing marijuana is just the most recent anti-mafia move in the USA, and not the last one.

Hopefully understanding just what Trump is talking about will make it better for everyone. Trump is talking about a political process which is designed to give the illusion of a voice that matters to the ordinary voters, when in reality what that system delivers is the agenda of the globalising governing elite. The U.S. system gives the illusion of choice to the non-elites, allowing them to generate one of two equally acceptable outcomes to the global governing elite, and that limited choice is biased in many ways, not just by money, in favor of the **preferred** acceptable outcome. Had republican élites forced the selection of Cruz instead of Trump as their candidate that would have been seen by Trump's base as exactly the kind of corruption that he (and the tea party) oppose, splitting the republican voters in the event of Trump campaigning as an independent. Cruz would not win, Trump likely would not have won either. Likewise, Trump's base would *also* perceive an impeachment of Trump as a betrayal by the globalizing elites against their own interests, which they naturally identify as "American".

Essentially I would regard everything Trump is saying about the economy with a large amount of skepticism. Then again, that's what people thought about Hitler.

The U.S. Supreme Court is inhabited entirely by the global governing elite. As we saw back in 2000 the global governing elite has a stranglehold on democracy and can select its preferred candidate even over the voice of a majority of voters in the face of obvious voting fraud done by computer (Diebold) and voter intimidation ("driving while black"). That backfired on them on 9/11 and continued to backfire till 2008.

To truly understand U.S. foreign policy and how factors beyond even the power of the U.S. President will constrain Trump for ever implementing the majority of his platform we now look at U.S. global hegemony.

C. U.S. Global Hegemony

What is <u>hegemony?</u>

<u>Hegemony</u> is the rulership over a region wherein the hegemon orders and governs the relations between and among suzerein states, states which are in alliance and close cooperation with the hegemon. It is a form of coordination of the governance of states.

<u>Since 1945 the U.S. has been the hegemon of the Western alliance.</u> And thereby the world. Marcus Tullius Cicero once said:

 "Our Roman Republic, by defending its allies, has got possession of the entire earth".

Thus it is with America, the new Rome. Since 1979 the United States has been increasingly in a positive hegemonic relationship with the People's Republic of China. From 1990 to 2001 the U.S. was global hegemon. However, since 2003 Russia is increasingly trying to break U.S. global hegemony, and is no longer cooperating with the U.S. in global governance.

Under what circumstances could U.S. global hegemony be broken?

There are absolutely people who would like to destroy U.S. global hegemony: <u>Vladimir Putin</u> is one such person.

<u>Putin consistently preaches and praises a so-called "multi-polar world"</u>. However, history shows repeatedly that <u>a multi-polar world is a world of constant wars.</u> In his efforts to

end U.S. global hegemony Putin tries to form an alliance of
<u>BRICs</u>: Brazil, Russia, India, China.

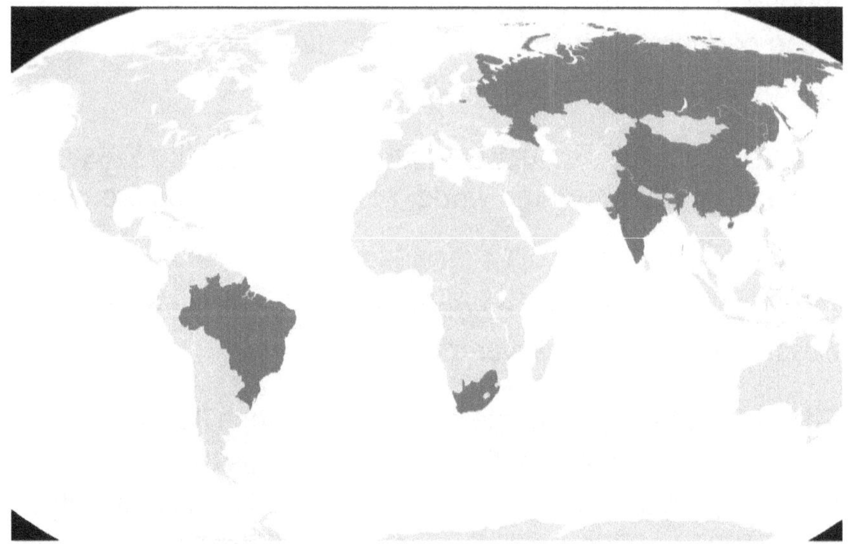

The BRICs are hardly a cohesive alliance: there is no
common ideology, history, or culture to unite the BRICs
around. The BRICs are characterized by corruption,
authoritarianism, and sometimes both. Thus, it is very
unlikely that an "axis of weasels" could topple U.S.
hegemony. However, Putin likely believes that he can
manipulate the issues and relations among these putative
allies to Russia's advantage. Unfortunately for Putin, the
Chinese leadership likely already knows that a) it does not
need Putin b) Putin does not propose a governance style
which is either apt for China or useful in China's own desire
to expand its economy and increase its political influence.
Putin, unlike the United States, has very little to offer China.

This does not mean that U.S. hegemony is unbreakable. It merely means that Putin will not be able to break it using an alliance of the BRICs.

Are there other examples of people opposing U.S. hegemony? In fact, yes. Osama Bin Laden is another person who wished to break U.S. global hegemony.

Bin Laden's stated aim was to quite literally bankrupt the United States by luring the United States into endless expensive wars which would bankrupt the U.S. treasury and ruin the U.S. alliance system.
It is worth pointing out that Bin Laden is dead, and the NATO alliance is not.

Given that there are in fact people who wish to destroy U.S. hegemony it is logical to ask whether and under what conditions U.S. hegemony could be destroyed.

U.S. global hegemony is based on: 1) a powerful economy, 2) an attractive culture of inclusion and freedom, and 3) the rule of law, not men. These three pillars of power may be simplistically referred to was **"Wall Street"**, **"Hollywood"**, and **"the Courts"**.

As a result of these three pillars of power the U.S. attracts 1) millions of hard-working, talented, intelligent **immigrants** 2) **capital**, the important material bases of U.S. power.

How might these pillars of power or their consequence be broken?

As long as the U.S. remains a state governed by the rule of law it will be extremely difficult to destroy U.S. power.

As long as the U.S. remains an open-society governed by the rule of law, a credit-worthy country, it will continue to attract millions of productive immigrants and form trillions of dollars of capital. If however the U.S. courts were corrupted or U.S. credit-worthiness degraded it would no longer attract and form massive capital.

The United States is noteworthy in that <u>the United States has never defaulted on its public debt.</u> This fact of non-default is quite unique: <u>there are very few countries which have never defaulted.</u> All of them are rich, and attract capital and that is no coincidence.

This means that the United States bonds are one of, even the most secure debt obligation investment, and thus pay a very low, even the lowest, rate of interest. That in turn means the U.S. can attract capital cheaply and makes the United States a magnet for capital formation.

Of course, if you wish to invest in Greek or Argentinian or Russian bonds you will have a higher rate of return - in theory. In practice, all three of those countries are the most notable examples of countries with irresponsible fiscal policies of debt and default, which lead in turn to a terribly poor economy. The last Russian debt default was in 1998, just prior to Putin's taking power. The next one will be just prior to Putin's leaving power. Such is the fate of countries where conquest and corruption is the governance style.

In order to maintain the credit of U.S. Treasury Bonds as the most secure government bond on earth the United States must do only two things, perhaps even only one: 1) maintain a steady flow of immigrants 2) not default on its debts, i.e. keep it's word.

I) *To maintain the credit of U.S. Treasury Bonds as the most secure government bond on earth* the United States must must maintain a steady flow of immigrants because immigrants are the productive base of the U.S. economy.

Marxists believe, wrongly, that the U.S. got so wealthy by ruthlessly exploiting the planet. Please. In fact, U.S.

exploitation of slaves and indigenous natives was costlier than cooperation, which is why slavery was abolished. Genocide is unproductive because dead people do not work. Slavery is unproductive because slaves have no incentive to work. Thus, rather than exploitation, the United States pursued policies of cooperation and integration within a free market economy of political liberalism. The result? Mass prosperity. The fact that slavery and conquest are expensive and unprofitable is the material explanation for the end of slavery and the integration of all races in the U.S. body politic. Moreover, inter-racial cooperation always predominated even in the colonial era. Cooperation and integration ultimately prevailed, because racial harmony is more productive, profitable, and enjoyable, a better way to live. Who wishes to live in an apartheid state?

Despite the fact that immigrants are desirable, even perhaps necessary for the United States economy, Trump threatens to cut off that steady stream of productive labor. In practice he will be unable to do so, fortunately. Even if the neo-nativist Trump were able to end all immigration the result would only be economic impoverishment and no great loss in military power.

Marxists are also wrong to think that the suddenly impoverished white workers in the U.S.A. would rebel and strike to gain state power: they already have state power. White workers who support the United States are not examples of false consciousness. They simply correctly recognize that the interests of the United States and their own self-interest generally align.

So, even if Trump were able to cut off the U.S. supply of immigrants --immigrants the United States needs to be able to compete with China-- I do not believe that, alone, would destroy the credit worthiness of the U.S. Dollar and the U.S. Treasury Bond. That would of course weaken the United States credit worthiness and the value of the dollar -- maybe Trump is a gold-bug, a commodity fetishist of gold? However, even cutting off all immigrants would likely not destroy the credit-worthiness of the United States. Two world wars, one civil war, and numerous economic crashes never resulted in a U.S. bond default: that is how powerful U.S. credit is. Even if a serial bankrupt fraudster has taken the office of the President with foreign intelligence collusion the U.S. rule of law culture and free-market ideology is sufficiently strong enough to vomit up the poison which is destroying the republican party from within.

II) *To maintain the credit of U.S. Treasury Bonds as the most secure government bond on earth* the United States must continue to pay its debts when they fall due as it has done for over 200 years. In other words, to maintain the credit of U.S. Treasury Bonds as the most secure government bond on earth the United States must merely continue to keep its word.

The United States has built a global world-order in which it is hegemon based on three factors:
1) The productivity of the American people.
2) The capacity to attract hard-working and intelligent immigrants.
3) The ability to attract capital.
I address these three factors in that order.

First: Productivity. The American people are among the hardest working people on this planet. That is not because of their race, for they are multiracial, so this is not a racist or chauvinist statement. It is simply a fact: people in the U.S. generally work hard, putting in more hours than people in other advanced capitalist countries.

Why are Americans so hard working?

Americans work so hard because their property is secure from expropriation, because their court system is not corrupt. They work so hard because it pays, and the harder they work the more it pays. Kleptocracies - countries led by a political class which loots and steals whether by taxes, confiscation, devaluation, bond default, or bribery - those countries are poor. Countries where the courts and cops are corrupt are poor. Countries which are poor are poor not because of exploitation by the prudent investors who defer consumption to take advantage of the time-value of money: otherwise Singapore and Germany would still be poor. Countries which are poor are poor because of corruption and kleptocracy.

Second: Immigrants. Why does the U.S. attract hard-working, talented, intelligent immigrants? The U.S. attracts so many hard-working, talented, intelligent immigrants because those immigrants know they will be enjoying a rule-of-law culture where their property will not be stolen and where they will be treated fairly by the courts. America attracts immigrants because it is attractive, especially in comparison with corrupt kleptocracies.

Third: Capital. Why does the United States attract and form literally trillions of dollars of capital, whether as investment in U.S. Treasury Bonds, shares in the U.S. stock market, or in U.S. real estate? The answer, again, is: the rule of law. Modest taxation, no expropriation, freedom of investment, a stable monetary policy, and responsible fiscal policies explain why the United States is a magnet for capital.

Given these material factors of U.S. power, all the United States has to do to maintain its global hegemeony is to continue its record of never having defaulted on its foreign debt.

It is perhaps no accident that President Trump, "the Manchurian President", has systematically threatened each of these pillars of power. Fortunately for the U.S. – and the global rule of law – even a U.S. President cannot destroy these bases of U.S. Power. The U.S., having been formed as the result of a revolution, was conceived "from the ground up" to guaranty individual freedoms, particularly among them property rights, the rule of law, not men, and to prevent a concentration of power whether in any branch of government or at the federal or state levels. U.S. Power is distributed and decentralized, a headless dragon.

Ultimately, it is President Trump's efforts to systematically undermine these pillars of American financial, cultural, and ideological power which would result in him being indicted and impeached for tax evasion, money laundering and possibly for other crimes such as human trafficking, obstruction of justice, racketeering, and conspiracy to

commit some or all of the aforementioned crimes; perhaps
also violations of the espionage act.

III. TRUMP AND NIXON

When I compare Trump to Nixon I mean this in several ways. Trump carried states Republicans usually lose such as Michigan and Wisconsin. He handily beat Clinton in traditional swing states like Pennsylvania and Ohio. Trump has realigned Republican ideology from global free-trade and open immigration to economic nationalism and foreign policy realism. This ideological realignment carried with it a demographic realignment which explains why Trump won in states which had been at least contested, even out-right democratic. This ideological shift in the republicans might well outlast Trump's term of office, since it won him the white house. Trump's ideology of state economic intervention and economic nationalism nicely parallels Nixon's views and policies.

As well as policy shifts Trump represents a fundamental ideological and demographic realignment as great as the one worked by Franklin Roosevelt. Yet, at the same time, Trump also faces the cloud of potential scandal. Trump could be the America's next Nixon in the unfortunate sense.

Trump is ideologically much like Nixon. Nixon, like Trump, was an economic nationalist. Like Nixon, Trump favors an interventionist role for the government in the economy. Nixon, recall, undertook wage and price restrictions, regulatory moves which would be unthinkable in the Washington consensus economic neo-liberalism which has dominated the beltway since 1990. Nixon was perfectly happy to negotiate with labor unions, for he correctly saw the American workers as generally speaking good patriots, solid hard-working Americans. Like Trump, Nixon justified and guided his economic and foreign policy interventions by the national interest. Nixon had no problem with a semi-planned economy with strong labor unions when that served the national interest. Trump and Nixon are both economic nationalists and economic interventionists. They are more-or-less both corporatists. Corporatism, roughly, is the idea that governance occurs through the mediation between corporations and labor unions: that the government should mediate the conflicts between labor and capital managing them in the interests of the nation. It is a form of economic nationalism, and is not inconsistent with mercantilism. This shift in republican ideology may also outlast Trump's term of office.

Trump is not only ideologically Nixon 2.0 -- he may also prove to have his own Watergate 2.0. Like Nixon, Trump may wind up being impeached and removed from office, whether for money laundering, tax evasion, obstruction of justice, violations of the Racketeer Influenced and Corrupt Organization Act, and perhaps even violations of the espionage act prior to his entry and into office and conspiracy to commit any of the above named offenses. These allegations, if true, might be even worse than Nixon's political tinkering and Nixon's attempt to create a de facto one-party state, since Nixon's wrong-doing did not involve cooperation with a hostile foreign intelligence service. This raises, at least in theory, the legal question of defenses which the President might raise or interpose in the defense of "all the President's men" such as his former campaign manager Paul Manafort or Mike Flynn. Let's suppose Trump or some of his staffers are guilty of some or all of the scandalous accusations swirling about the Trump administration. What defenses might Trump raise or interpose?

A. PRESIDENTIAL PARDON DEFENSE

One defense which the President might interpose or raise is the Presidential power to pardon crimes. Although the U.S. President can indeed pardon *federal* crimes the President's pardon power is limited to *federal* crimes. The President has no power to pardon state crimes. It is an interesting question whether the President can pardon violations of international law. Given the President's role as chief executor of U.S. foreign policy it is probably the case that the President can indeed pardon a violation of international law, albeit foreign states are obviously not bound by such Presidential pardons and such pardon, e.g. of a jus cogens violation, might be a breach of U.S. obligations under international law. Thereto, the U.S. president obviously has no power to pardon violations of the laws of foreign countries; if the President has the power to pardon a prosecution of a foreign law before a U.S. court, the application of foreign laws in U.S. federal courts, this too would in no way limit the right and power of a foreign country to enforce it's own laws against such defendant. Finally, the President cannot self-pardon. The constitution specifically provides a process for the impeachment of a President. If the President could self-pardon then no President could ever be impeached as a practical fact. That would obviate the impeachment process, making an operative portion of the constitution inoperative: constitutional provisions are presumed to have at least executory effect. Some argue that a President cannot pardon indicted co-conspirators: that is a fine question. The President cannot self-pardon but to pardon one member of a conspiracy is not to pardon every conspirator and thus the better views is that the President can pardon their co-conspirators. These are all however but theoretical legal questions, at least at present.

B. SUPREMACY CLAUSE DEFENSE

Some commentators appear to believe, to my view wrongly, that the Supremacy clause of the U.S. constitution means that the President cannot be criminally accused for violations of state law by one of the several states. That view misapprehends the nature of sovereignty in the federation. While Federal law is indeed supreme as to state law in those areas of concurrent sovereignty, those places where each sovereign may legislate, there must be an intention by the federation in its legislation to preempt, i.e. to entirely displace, state law. The party pleading preemption must bear the burden of proving that the federation intended to displace all state law in that field. In doubt, there will be no finding of preemption. As to the federal power, federal criminal power is exceptional and must be proven. In contrast, state capacity to legislate criminal law is presumed. The police power of the federation is limited to areas of interstate and international commerce as well as to foreign relations. In contrast, state police power is limited only by fundamental rights of the U.S. constitution. This too explains why, federal anti-money laundering law does not displace state anti-money laundering law, for one example.

Under *international* law the head of state is immune for all acts during their term of office: heads of state might not be immune for jus cogens violations under international law during their term of office but certainly are after their term expires. Head of State immunity ends as to unofficial acts of the Head of State after their term of office. International crimes are obviously not official acts, a fortiori violations of jus cogens (say, bombarding civilians with chemical weapons in Aleppo, for one example). Thus, a sitting President cannot be judged before a *foreign* court. After the term of office expires however a foreign court may adjudicate a former President for unofficial acts which were crimes they committed during their term of office. That is the extent of Presidential immunity, and no further.

Although *international* law provides for the immunity of the head of state during his or her term of office that is not the case under U.S. domestic law. U.S. domestic law provides no criminal immunity for the President: the President is immune in tort, not crime, for their official acts, only, during their term of office. After the expiry of the President's term of office the former President is only immune in tort for their official acts.

Under U.S. domestic law the U.S. President enjoys no immunity as to unofficial acts, i.e. crimes, even during their term of office. This is because the U.S. constitution is not a treaty between sovereign states but an organic act of the constituent people (White settlers, Black freemen and slaves, civilized Indians and their descendants and immigrants). U.S. constitutional rights and duties are not derived from international law but are expressed by the popular will of the American citizenry. Hence, if there were any Presidential immunity it must appear in the constitution itself and not by implication from international law.

We can see that the U.S. President does not enjoy criminal immunity in the constitution itself. Nowhere does the constitution provide for presidential immunity. Quite the opposite, the U.S. constitution provides that the head of state "shall be removed from Office on Impeachment for, and Conviction of, Treason, Bribery, or other high Crimes and Misdemeanors": *shall*, not *may*: this is an obligation, not an option. A seated president could not be convicted and then removed from office were s/he immune. Consequently, there is no criminal immunity for the President of the United States during their term of office.

Some legal commentators and political pundits appear to be taking Nixon's line on so-called presidential immunity, a line he most likely got from Kissinger. Of course, German constitutional law (and Kissinger was born in Germany) does provide for head of state immunity in domestic law. This is because the German state formed as a treaty arrangement between independent countries and thereafter was destroyed by two world wars featuring all varieties of official criminality: to maintain the social peace and to prevent selective prosecution the German Chancellor and Members of the German Parliament enjoy a certain immunity which, fortunately, has become less relevant in the past decades.

Consequently, the "Presidential immunity" defense did not work for Nixon, and likewise would not work for President

Trump were he indicted for various federal or state crimes. The US Constitution is an organic act of the American people, not an treaty.

CONCLUSION: THE WAY FORWARD

Trump's Presidency represents a radical break in bi-partisan consensus on key issues facing the American Republic. The rise of Trump also represents a fundamental shift in political focus of the main parties. The challenges Trump reflects and represents may shatter either or both political parties. Trump's insights and innovations, regardless of his flaws or friends, have brought to the fore-front issues which will continue to define U.S. politics in the next decade or even decades, regardless of his personal fate or success at implementing his program.

Trump represents the return of corporatism. Corporatism regards the role of the state as mediating conflicts between labor and capital to articulate and attain the national interest. Corporatism thus sees an interventionist role for the state. Likewise, corporatism is a nationalist ideology, not a globalist or internationalist one. Trump has shown the major parties that there is a large sector of voters, mostly from the de-industrialized states, who have been materially injured by the destruction of U.S. industries resulting from globalization and free trade. However, Trump fails to understand that the reason these industries were destroyed is that the U.S. labor force is uncompetitive. US labor is less well-educated and perhaps less disciplined than European or Japanese labor. At the same time, it is much more expensive than labor from e.g. China, India, and the rest of the developing world generally. Yet, the U.S.A. cannot and will not offer any social democratic retraining programs or social welfare benefits to the disempowered hand-workers and former industrial employees. The U.S. cannot and will not implement a European style social democracy with strong labor protections and plenty of welfare benefits funded by social insurance payments and much higher sales taxes ("value added taxes"). There are many reasons the U.S.A. cannot and will not construct a European style social democratic welfare state:

First, the U.S. is a multination country of immigrants. Consequently, there is an insufficient sense of compassion and responsibility among recipients of state aid to generate the political will and social benefits of a welfare state.

Second, the U.S.A. was founded on a tax revolt: U.S. people hate paying taxes. They especially hate paying taxes which fund different ethnic groups than their own. Above all they despise paying taxes to fund different ethnic groups which are perceived, rightly or wrongly as "lazy" "criminal" "entitled" "whiners".

Third, the U.S.A. has an ideology of individualism and capitalism: if you are poor in the U.S.A. most people think it is your own fault, that you deserve it, and need to lift yourself up by your own bootstraps rather than relying on strangers' (largely absent) compassion. Thus, the U.S. has and will continue to have homelessness, crime driven by desperation, and soup kitchens and food banks administered by Churches (never Synagogues, by the way): the "salivation army". Since the U.S.A. cannot and will not implement anything like a European social democracy it will keep having the highest rate of incarceration on the planet.

The only answer, the only logical way forward to meet these challenges, is to legally and politically empower trade unions. Government must task trade unions with social welfare functions like labor (re-)training, homeless shelter construction, renovation, and administration, as well as soup kitchen construction and administration. Government must also link labor unions to local primary education (schools) through shop and laboratory courses, apprenticeships, and Vocational Technology programs such as BOCES and to make clear that these practical programs will lead to solid jobs and career opportunities should the VoTech student wish to go on to community college for book-work instead of hand-work. Electricians, plumbers, construction workers, chefs, janitors, are all necessary stable work which *cannot* be outsourced. Whether the USA can re-industrialize with high-technology is a good question but even if it could those highly skilled jobs are exactly the ones which Trump's disempowered unintellectual base is least likely to want or even have an aptitude for. Social bodies such as Churches and Synagogues, charities and trade unions schools and foundations must be expressly granted quasi-governance functions to provide the social welfare protections needed to have a productive industrial economy. Germany and Japan already ate Detroit's lunch. Seattle is next. Part of why they did so is because of their labor laws and policies.

Ultimately Trump is a reaction to the destruction of American industry and of the American labor movement, the looting and betrayal of American workers by Goldman-Sachs, Madoff, Facebook, AIG etc. The rise of a cynical, dishonest, and unpatriotic oligarchy of billionaires in the USA who care only about their money and not the nation or the citizen isn't evidence of American success. It's the harbinger of the destruction of the republic.

In that sense, the scapegoater Trump, who likes to blame immigrants, may well end up himself a scapegoat: a scapegoat of traitors and oligarchs.

OTHER BOOKS BY ERIC ENGLE

Eric Engle has written and edited dozens of books reviewing all basic law courses and the actual questions from the 1992 and 1999 bar exams, released by the NCBEx. Available at:

http://amazon.com/author/quizmaster

He also offers free law review articles online and free online search engines for US, French, German, Russian and International law at:

http://mindworks.altervista.org

Can You Do Me A Big Favour?

If you enjoyed this book, found it useful or otherwise then I'd really appreciate it if you would post a short review on Amazon. I read all reviews personally so I can improve the product. You can write me an email if eric.engle@yahoo.com to ask me specific questions or for clarifications. cannot promise to answer. This gratuitous offer for Q&A entails nor implies any legal obligations - there is no contractually included after-sales service here. You want to learn and I love to teach, feel free to write.

Thank you for your support!